Wild Weather

Jacqueline Martin

Contents

OXFORD
UNIVERSITY PRESS

OXFORD
UNIVERSITY PRESS

Great Clarendon Street, Oxford OX2 6DP

Oxford University Press is a department of the University of Oxford. It furthers the University's objective of excellence in research, scholarship, and education by publishing worldwide in

Oxford New York

Auckland Cape Town Dar es Salaam Hong Kong Karachi Kuala Lumpur Madrid Melbourne Mexico City Nairobi New Delhi Shanghai Taipei Toronto

With offices in

Argentina Austria Brazil Chile Czech Republic France Greece Guatemala Hungary Italy Japan Poland Portugal Singapore South Korea Switzerland Thailand Turkey Ukraine Vietnam

OXFORD and OXFORD ENGLISH are registered trade marks of Oxford University Press in the UK and in certain other countries

ISBN: 978 0 19 464498 3

An Audio CD Pack containing this book and a CD is also available, ISBN 978 0 19 464538 6

The CD has a choice of American and British English recordings of the complete text.

An accompanying Activity Book is also available, ISBN 978 0 19 464508 9

Printed in China

This book is printed on paper from certified and well-managed sources.

ACKNOWLEDGEMENTS

Illustrations by: Kelly Kennedy pp.5, 9, 15, 17, 22, 31; Ian Moores pp.4, 8, 10, 15, 16, 32, 38; Dusan Pavlic/Beehive Illustration pp.36, 44; Alan Rowe pp.36, 44.

The Publishers would also like to thank the following for their kind permission to reproduce photographs and other copyright material: Alamy pp.12 (Jason Smalley/Wildspace/stratus, A.T.Willett/cumulus, FB Rose/imagebroker/cirrus), 13 (Andrzej Gorzkowski Photography), 26 (Andrew McConnell), 35 (Charles Crust/Danita Delimont, Agent/solar panels); Corbis pp.7 (Staffan Widstrand), 9 (Fridmar Damm), 19 (Jayanta Shaw/Reuters), 20 (Galen Rowell/Latitude), 22 (Visuals Unlimited), 30 (Jim Reed Photography), 35 (Hashimoto Noboru/Corbis Sygma/solar boat); Getty Images pp.11 (Alan Copson/Photographer's Choice), 18 (Sebastian D'Souza/AFP), 27 (Peter Turner/Stone); Oxford University Press pp.3, 5, 6, 14, 23, 24, 25, 28, 29, 34; Photolibrary p.21 (Mark Cassino/Superstock); Science Photo Library p.17 (Simon Fraser); Still Pictures p.33 (Biosphoto/Vernay Pierre/Polar Lys).

With thanks to: Ann Fullick for science checking

Introduction

Wind, rain, cloud, and snow are all types of weather. Weather is different in different places around the world. In some places the weather is the same every day, and in other places it changes every hour. Weather can be calm or wild!

What are these types of weather called?
Do you know what places have these types of weather?
What types of weather are there where you live?

Discover!
Now read and discover more about different types of weather!

What Is Weather?

Around Earth, there is a blanket of air called the atmosphere. Weather is the different conditions in the atmosphere. What types of weather do you like?

How Does Weather Happen?

Most of the weather on Earth happens because of two things – the sun, and air pressure. The sun heats some parts of Earth more than others, so air is warmer in some places and cooler in others. Areas of warm or cold air, called air masses, move around and bring different types of weather. When two masses meet, the weather changes.

You can't feel it, but the air is pushing down on you. This is called air pressure. Air pressure can change. Low air pressure brings rain and wind. High air pressure brings clear skies, which means hot, sunny days in summer, but cold days in winter.

Air Masses Meeting

rain clouds

warm air mass

cold air mass

Knowing About the Weather

We need to know about the weather so that we can build the right type of homes, wear the right clothes, and travel at the right time. If people on ships and planes know about the weather, they can avoid bad storms. If farmers know about the weather, they can plant and cut down crops at the right time.

In 1992, weather forecasters warned people in the USA that Hurricane Andrew was coming. Sadly, 54 people died, but lots of people survived.

Discover!

In the past, the Chippewa Indians in North America thought that the sun was in a bag all winter. They believed that every spring, a mouse bit a hole in the bag and the sun came out!

Predicting the Weather

A good way to predict the weather is to look at the types of cloud in the sky. Today, scientists use computers to predict the weather, but in the past, people watched nature. They watched what happened to plants, animals, the moon, or the stars. Many people still do this.

Some people think that cows or sheep can predict the weather. They think that if animals sit down, it will rain. People also believe that a red sky at night means good weather the next day, but a red sky in the morning means bad weather.

Many years ago, scientists flew in hot-air balloons to measure the weather. Today, they collect information from weather stations, weather planes, weather balloons, and satellites, to understand what the weather will do. Millions of measurements are taken every day. The information helps scientists to predict the weather.

A Weather Station

weather balloon

Discover!

There are about 10,000 weather stations around the world.

Go to pages 36–37 for activities.

World Weather

Weather can be very different around the world depending on the climate and the landscape. The climate is the usual weather for a place. The landscape is what the land is like.

Weather and Climate

Weather can change, but climates stay the same most of the time. There are different types of climate because of the sun. The sun shines most strongly on the middle of Earth, called the equator. Places near the equator have hot climates with lots of hot, sunny weather. Places far from the equator have cold climates with cold, snowy weather. Places in between have temperate climates, where the weather is mild.

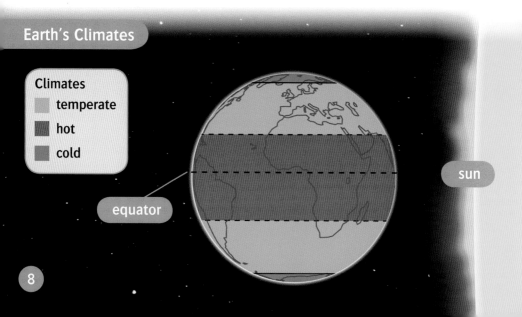

Earth's Climates

Climates
temperate
hot
cold

sun

equator

Adapting to Climate

Different things live and grow in different climates. Plants and animals adapt to where they live, for example, animals in cold climates often have thick coats to keep them warm.

Only plants with short roots can grow in cold climates because the ground is frozen for most of the year.

Very few plants can grow in deserts because there isn't enough water. Cactus plants survive because they can store water.

Discover!

If lightning hits a cactus, it can explode. The lightning boils the water inside the cactus and the steam makes part of the cactus explode!

Saguaro Cactus Plants

Weather and Seasons

Earth goes around the sun. For some of the year, one half of Earth is nearer the sun, so it has warmer weather called summer. At the same time, the other half is away from the sun, so it has colder weather called winter. This is how the seasons work.

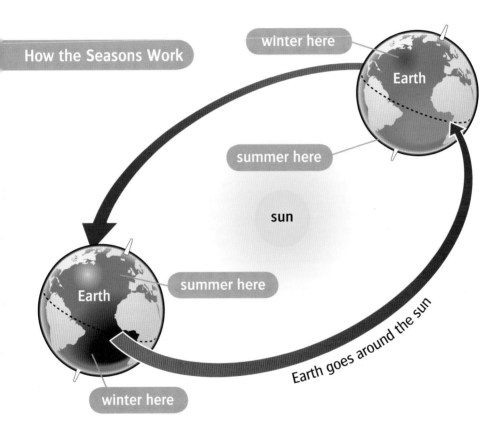

How the Seasons Work

winter here

Earth

summer here

sun

summer here

Earth

winter here

Earth goes around the sun

Most places have summer and winter, but in temperate climates there are also seasons called spring and fall, when the weather isn't as hot as summer or as cold as winter. Places near the equator are usually hot, but they have wet and dry seasons.

Weather and Landscape

The weather of a place can change depending on the landscape. If you climb a mountain, the air gets about 6 degrees centigrade (°C) colder every 1,000 meters that you climb. So there can be snow at the top of a mountain near the equator!

Land gets warm faster than the ocean, so in summer, inland places are warmer than places near the ocean. Inland places cool down faster, too, so they are colder in winter.

The Plains in Arizona, USA

Discover! Plains have some of the hottest weather. They have hot summers, and cold, dry winters because they are far from the ocean and they can be protected by mountains, too.

Go to pages 38–39 for activities.

3 All About Clouds

Clouds look light, but even a small cloud can be as heavy as 100 elephants! Every cloud is made of millions of tiny drops of water.

Cloud Shapes

There are many cloud shapes, but they all come from three types of cloud. If we look at the type of cloud in the sky, this can help us to predict the weather.

Stratus clouds are low, thin blankets of cloud. These can bring light rain. Cumulus clouds usually bring good weather, but if they get too big or low they can change into cumulonimbus clouds – and that means storms! Cirrus clouds form high in the sky. They are made of ice crystals and they often mean that bad weather is coming.

stratus clouds

cumulus clouds

cirrus clouds

Mist and Fog

At night the ground cools down and it also cools the air above it. When the air gets cold, the water in it can turn into mist. Mist is like a very thin cloud.

Fog is like mist, but it's a thicker cloud that forms nearer the ground. It's very hard to see in fog and you can easily get lost, so it can be dangerous. Driving in fog is also dangerous, but cars have special fog lights to help other drivers to see them.

Storm Clouds

When hot air rises on a hot day, it can change into storm clouds. In a storm, strong winds make the tiny drops of water inside clouds hit each other, and this makes electricity. The electricity moves between the cloud and the ground, and it makes very bright flashes of light called lightning. Lightning is about 30,000 degrees centigrade! Lightning heats the air around it, and the air moves away very fast and makes a loud noise called thunder. There are about 40,000 thunderstorms every day!

Discover!

Light travels faster than sound, so you see lightning before you hear thunder. Count the seconds between lightning and thunder. If you count three seconds, the storm is a kilometer away.

A Thunderstorm

Lightning Facts!

There are many different types of lightning. Forked lightning and zigzag lightning are the most common, but there are also sheet lightning and rocket lightning.

forked lightning

zigzag lightning

sheet lightning

rocket lightning

About 100 lightning flashes happen every second on Earth, but most of them don't hit the ground. Lightning usually hits tall things like trees and buildings. The Empire State Building in New York in the USA is hit by lightning about 100 times every year. Lightning doesn't usually hit people, but a park ranger in Virginia in the USA has been hit seven times!

Discover!

Lightning is almost six times hotter than the sun. It can even melt rock!

Go to pages 40–41 for activities.

4 Here Comes the Rain

People, animals, and plants all need water. Enough rain falls every day for 100 baths for every person on Earth! Sadly, some people don't have enough water because more rain falls in some places than others.

What Is Rain?

Rain is water that falls from clouds onto the ground and into rivers, lakes, and oceans. When the sun heats the water, some of the water changes into a gas called water vapor. This is called evaporation. Water vapor rises into the sky where it cools and changes back into tiny drops of water that make clouds. The drops of water get bigger and then they fall as rain. Rainwater goes into rivers, rivers go into lakes and oceans, and the process starts again. This is called the water cycle.

The Water Cycle

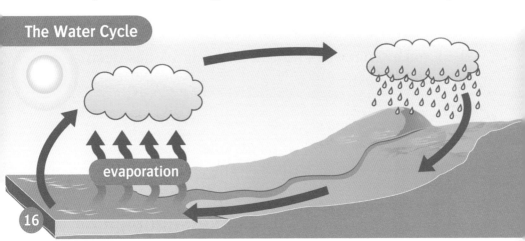

evaporation

Rainbows

When there is rain and sun at the same time, raindrops break light from the sun into different colors and we see a rainbow. There are seven different colors in a rainbow – red, orange, yellow, green, blue, indigo, and violet. Sometimes you can see two or more rainbows in the sky at the same time. You can only see a rainbow if you are between the sun and the rain.

Have you ever seen a rainbow at night? Rainbows made in the light from the moon are called moonbows!

Discover! If you see a rainbow from a plane, it will look like a circle.

Monsoons

In tropical climates, where it's hot and wet, there are only two seasons. For half of the year, winds blow from the land to the ocean and there is a hot, dry season. For the other half of the year, winds blow from the ocean to the land and there is a long, wet season. When the winds change, and they blow from the ocean, it's called the monsoon. Monsoon winds bring heavy rain. People need monsoon rain for their crops to grow, but it can bring problems, too.

Discover! One of the wettest places on Earth is Cherrapunji in India. About 11.5 meters of rain falls there every year!

Is Rain Good or Bad?

We need rain to help things grow, but if there is heavy rain, rivers sometimes overflow and make floods. Floods can happen anywhere, even in deserts. Floods can destroy buildings and crops, and they can kill animals and people. Floods can be good, too. The mud from a flood makes soil more fertile, so crops grow better.

In Bangladesh, there are floods after the monsoon almost every year. Bangladesh has the most fertile soil in the world!

A Flooded Village, Bangladesh

Go to pages 42–43 for activities.

5 Cold Weather

About 11,000 years ago, more than 30% of Earth was covered in ice! Earth is warmer today, but we still have cold weather.

Where Is It Cold?

The coldest climates on Earth are near the North and South Poles. Most of the ice there never melts. Some ice has been there for more than two million years!

The coldest place in the world is Vostok in Antarctica. The temperature there is usually about minus 57 degrees centigrade, but in 1987 it reached minus 89 degrees. That's the coldest temperature ever recorded!

Snow and Sleet

When the air temperature is less than 0 degrees centigrade, water drops in the clouds change into ice crystals. As more drops freeze, the crystals get bigger. Then, as the crystals fall through the clouds, they hit each other and form snowflakes.

Snow can be fun, but it can make it difficult for people to travel. When it's cold, you must keep your hands, toes, and nose warm or they can go numb. If you get too cold you can get hypothermia – this is when your body is so cold that it stops working.

If the temperature near the ground is more than 0 degrees centigrade, snowflakes start to melt and they change into sleet. Sleet is a mixture of rain and snow.

Snowflakes

Discover!

All snowflakes have six parts, but every one has a different pattern.

layer

Hailstones

Hail

When air rises and carries water drops up to where
the air freezes, the drops freeze and form hailstones.
Small hailstones start to fall, but they are pushed up
again by more rising air, and another layer of ice
forms on top of the hailstone. This keeps happening
until the hailstones are heavier than the air, and
then they fall to the ground. If you cut a hailstone in
half, you can count how many times this happened
by counting the layers of ice!

Discover!

Most hailstones are
very small, but the biggest
hailstone ever recorded was
almost 18 centimeters wide.
That's as big as a soccer ball!

Blizzards

A heavy snowstorm with icy winds and temperatures less than minus 12 degrees centigrade is called a blizzard. Blizzards can happen very quickly and the snow can cover buildings, cars, and trains. Power cables can fall down, leaving people in their homes with no electricity.

In a strong blizzard you can't see where the sky meets the ground. This is called a whiteout. In whiteouts, planes can crash and birds can fly into the ground!

Heavy snow can also make avalanches happen – this is when a lot of snow falls down mountains very quickly. Avalanches cover everything as they move.

A Strong Blizzard

Go to pages 44–45 for activities.

6 Hot Weather

Weather is hottest in places near the equator because they are nearer the sun. Weather here can be hot and dry, or hot and wet. The highest temperature recorded was in Libya in 1922. It was 58 degrees centigrade!

Hot Deserts

Places with less than 25 centimeters of rain every year are called deserts. Deserts can be hot or cold, but they are almost always dry because the winds there blow from the land to the ocean. During the day, the skies are usually clear and sunny, but with no clouds to keep the heat in, the nights can be very cold!

The Atacama Desert, Chile

Discover!

The driest place in the world is the Atacama Desert in Chile. It once had no rain for 400 years!

Droughts and Fires

If rain doesn't fall for a long time, rivers and lakes can dry up. When this happens it's called a drought. Crops can't grow without water, so if there's a long drought, people don't have enough to eat and there can be a famine.

Hot sun can start fires. Fires can be a big problem in hot, dry countries because trees and other plants are dry. Forest fires are not always bad because they clear up dead leaves and help the soil. Some plants need strong heat for their seeds to grow!

A Sandstorm

Sandstorms

When storm clouds form after a hot day in the desert, sandstorms can happen. Most sandstorms are not dangerous and they are only a few meters high, but sometimes strong winds blow the sand up to 3 kilometers in the air and carry it for thousands of kilometers. Big sandstorms can break rocks and they can last for three or more days! It's difficult to see and breathe in a sandstorm.

Humid Weather

Hot places are not always dry. Hot places near water are often humid because air sucks up the water that evaporates from oceans and rivers. The amount of water vapor in the air is called its humidity.

In hot, humid weather your sweat can't evaporate, so you can't cool down. You must drink lots of water in hot weather. If your body gets too hot you can get heatstroke and be sick.

Discover! On a clear, humid day you can sometimes see the water vapor in the air – this is called a heat haze.

A Heat Haze

Go to pages 46–47 for activities.

As Earth moves, air moves with it. Warm air rises and cool air takes its place. As air moves, the pressure changes. Air goes from the high pressure to the low pressure, and this makes wind.

Types of Wind

Winds get their names from the direction that they blow from. For example, a north wind blows from north to south. We can see which direction a wind is blowing from by looking at a weathervane.

A Weathervane

west

south

north

east

28

eye

Storm Winds

Storm winds are called hurricanes over the Atlantic Ocean, cyclones over the Indian Ocean, and typhoons over the Pacific Ocean.

A hurricane starts as a thunderstorm over the ocean. The warm, wet air rises quickly and as Earth moves, it makes the storm spin upward. The center of a hurricane is called the eye – here the weather is calm, but around it there is heavy rain, and winds of up to 350 kilometers per hour. It's difficult to predict where hurricanes will go because they can change speed and direction very quickly. Hurricanes can last for a week!

Discover!

Since 1978, every hurricane has had a name. The strongest hurricane ever recorded is Hurricane Wilma.

29

Tornadoes

Tornadoes, or twisters, are the fastest winds on Earth. The storm clouds are a funnel shape, and they spin down from thunderclouds. When the tornado touches the ground, it starts to move like a vacuum cleaner, sucking up things from the ground. Tornadoes move quite slowly, at about 40 kilometers per hour, but winds inside the funnel can have speeds of up to 800 kilometers per hour! Tornadoes are much smaller than hurricanes and they usually only last a few minutes, but they are very strong!

Discover!

In 1986 some children in China were sucked up by a tornado that destroyed their school. They were put down safely 20 kilometers away!

Measuring the Wind

A British man called Francis Beaufort found a way to record the strength of the wind. This is called the Beaufort scale.

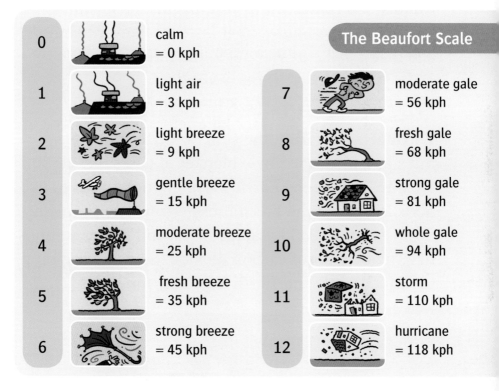

The Beaufort Scale

0		calm = 0 kph
1		light air = 3 kph
2		light breeze = 9 kph
3		gentle breeze = 15 kph
4		moderate breeze = 25 kph
5		fresh breeze = 35 kph
6		strong breeze = 45 kph
7		moderate gale = 56 kph
8		fresh gale = 68 kph
9		strong gale = 81 kph
10		whole gale = 94 kph
11		storm = 110 kph
12		hurricane = 118 kph

There are different scales to measure stronger winds, like tornadoes and hurricanes. These scales go from 1 to 5. Level 1 tornadoes can push cars off the road, and level 5 tornadoes can lift a house off the ground! Level 5 hurricanes can damage a lot of things, for example, they can pull up trees and destroy buildings. A really big hurricane can be as big as Australia!

→ Go to pages 48–49 for activities.

8 In the Future

Earth is getting warmer. The climate has become warmer and colder in the past, but scientists think that it's now getting warmer faster than ever before and that it will stay warmer in the future.

Why Is the Climate Changing?

Earth gets heat from the sun. Some heat escapes, but some is trapped by a blanket of gases like carbon dioxide. This keeps Earth warm enough for us to live here. It's called the greenhouse effect. The problem now is that our vehicles, factories, and power stations have made a lot of carbon dioxide. So we're trapping too much heat, and Earth is getting too warm!

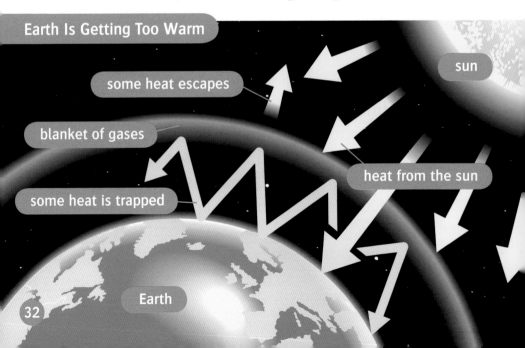

Earth Is Getting Too Warm

some heat escapes

sun

blanket of gases

heat from the sun

some heat is trapped

Earth

Weather in the Future

More heat means that there will be more rain, stronger winds, and storms in some places, and more droughts and famines in others. It also means that the snow and ice on mountains and around the Poles will melt, so sea levels will rise. If all the glaciers in the world melt, sea levels will rise more than 60 meters, and places near the ocean will go underwater! Ocean ice also helps keep Earth cool. If it melts, Earth will get even warmer!

What Can We Do?

It's probably too late to stop the climate changing, but we can help to slow it down. We must make less carbon dioxide to help to keep Earth cool. We can use our cars less – we can walk or ride a bicycle. We can also plant more trees. Trees use carbon dioxide to make food, so if there are more trees, there will be less carbon dioxide in the atmosphere.

Using Energy from the Weather

We need electricity, but we don't have to make it in power stations. Instead, we can make it from energy from the weather. Wind energy and solar energy are called green energy. Green energy makes less carbon dioxide.

To make electricity, we can use strong winds to turn windmills that power turbines. Lots of windmills together are called a wind farm. Wind farms are often on hills or out in the ocean because the winds are stronger there.

A Wind Farm

Solar panels can change light from the sun into electricity. This electricity can power small machines or heat homes. People use solar panels all around the world.

Solar Panels

The sun can even power cars and boats! Solar-powered vehicles can be expensive, but they don't make carbon dioxide. People keep finding new ways to use our amazing weather!

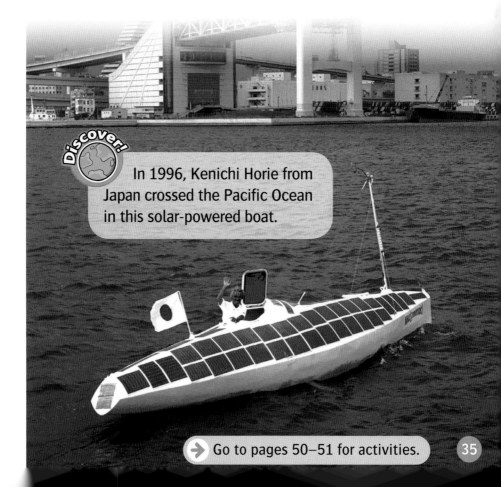

Discover!

In 1996, Kenichi Horie from Japan crossed the Pacific Ocean in this solar-powered boat.

Go to pages 50–51 for activities.

1 What Is Weather?

← Read pages 4–7.

1 Write the words.

sun   sky   moon   cloud   ~~rain~~   stars

1 ____rain____   2 _____   3 _____

4 _____   5 _____   6 _____

2 Circle the correct words.

1 Around Earth, there is a blanket of **water** / **air** called the atmosphere.

2 Weather is the different conditions in the **atmosphere** / **ocean**.

3 Most weather happens because of the **moon** / **sun**, and air pressure.

4 An area of warm or cold air is called an air **mass** / **pressure**.

5 The air is **falling** / **pushing** down on you.

6 **High** / **Low** air pressure brings rain and wind.

3 **Write complete sentences. Use these words.**

plant   avoid   ~~build~~   crops   ~~homes~~   storms   drive

1 We need to know about the weather, _so that we can_
   build the right type of homes.

2 Drivers need to know about the weather, _____

   _____

3 Farmers need to know about the weather, _____

   _____

4 Pilots need to know about the weather, _____

   _____

4 **Correct the sentences.**

1 A good way to predict the weather is to look at the stars.

   A good way to predict the weather is to look at
   the clouds.

2 Today, scientists use cows to predict the weather.

   _____

3 In the past, people watched food to predict the weather.

   _____

4 Some people think that if animals stand up, it will rain.

   _____

5 People believe that a red sky in the morning means
   good weather the next day.

   _____

2 World Weather

← Read pages 8–11.

equator   hot climates
cold climates   temperate climates

1 **Write the words.**

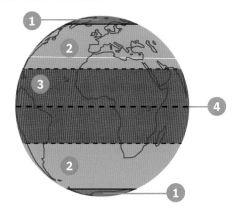

1 _____

2 _____

3 _____

4 _____

2 **Complete the chart. Write five more places.**

Hot Climate	Cold Climate	Temperate Climate
_____	_Antarctica_	_____
_____	_____	_____

3 **Write *weather* or *climate*.**

1 the usual weather for a place   _climate_

2 this changes all the time   _____

3 this stays the same most of the time   _____

4 there are different types of this
   because of the sun   _____

5 sun, rain, and snow are types of this _____

6 this changes every season   _____

4 **Complete the sentences.**

> winter   short   ~~animals~~   four
> spring   summer   water   coats

1 Plants and ___animals___ adapt to where they live.

2 Animals in cold climates have thick _____ to keep them warm.

3 Plants with _____ roots can grow in cold climates.

4 Few plants can grow in deserts because there isn't enough _____ .

5 We have colder weather in _____ .

6 We have warmer weather in _____ .

7 Temperate climates have _____ seasons.

8 The season after winter and before summer is called _____ .

5 **Order the words.**

1 place. / usual / a / climate / the / The / is / weather / for

   ___The climate is the usual weather for a place.___

2 warm / Land / ocean. / faster / gets / the / than

   _____

3 hottest / have / the / weather. / Plains

   _____

4 Plains / dry / have / winters. / summers / cold, / hot / and

   _____

3 All About Clouds

1 Match. Then write the sentences.

Cirrus clouds are	low, thin blankets of cloud.
Cumulus clouds are	thick cloud near the ground.
Stratus clouds are	made of ice crystals.
Mist is	clouds that often bring good weather.
Fog is	very thin cloud.

1 _Cirrus clouds are made of ice crystals._

2 _____

3 _____

4 _____

5 _____

2 Order the words.

1 elephants. A / can / cloud / be /as / heavy / 100 / as

_____

2 of / are / Clouds / of / millions / water. / of / made / drops

_____

3 many / different / shapes. / are / There /cloud

_____

3 Complete the sentences.

lightning   electricity   clouds
thunderstorms   thunder   tall

1 When hot air rises on a hot day, it can change into
   storm _____ .

2 Water drops inside clouds hit each other and this
   makes _____ .

3 Electricity from the cloud makes bright flashes of light
   called _____ .

4 When the hot air around lightning moves away, it
   makes _____ .

5 There are 40,000 _____ every day.

6 Lightning usually hits _____ things.

4 Answer the questions.

1 How can you know how far away a storm is?
   Count the seconds between lightning and thunder.

2 What are the most common types of lightning?
   _____

3 How often does lightning hit the Empire State Building?
   _____

4 How hot is lightning?
   _____

5 Have you ever seen a thunderstorm?
   _____

4 Here Comes the Rain

← Read pages 16–19.

**1 Write the colors in the correct order.
Then color the rainbow.**

yellow   ~~red~~   violet   green   orange   indigo   blue

1 ___red___

2 _____

3 _____

4 _____

5 _____

6 _____

7 _____

2 Complete the sentences.

animals   overflow   fertile   deserts   soil   year

1 If there is heavy rain, rivers sometimes _____ .

2 Floods can happen anywhere, even in _____ .

3 Floods can destroy crops and kill _____ .

4 In Bangladesh there are floods almost every _____ .

5 Mud from a flood makes soil more _____ .

6 Bangladesh has the most fertile _____ in
the world!

3 **Match. Then write the sentences.**

The sun heats	rivers and oceans.
Water vapor rises	the water.
Some water changes	and changes back into water.
Rain falls into	into the sky.
Drops of water fall	into water vapor.
Water vapor cools	from the clouds as rain.

1 _____

2 _____

3 _____

4 _____

5 _____

6 _____

4 **Answer the questions.**

1 How many seasons are there in tropical climates?

_____

2 Why do people need the monsoon rains?

_____

3 Write two things that floods can do.

_____

4 Have you ever seen a flood?

_____

5 Cold Weather

← Read pages 20–23.

1 Write the words.

snow   hail   sleet   ice

1 _____   2 _____   3 _____   4 _____

2 Match.

1 biggest hailstone ever recorded	0°C
2 parts of a snowflake	11,000 years ago
3 the temperature when water freezes	minus 89°C
4 30% of Earth covered in ice	two million years
5 some ice has been near the Poles	6
6 coldest temperature ever recorded	18 centimeters

3 Number the sentences in order.

Rising air carries water drops up into the sky. ☐ 1

Hailstones are pushed back up by the rising air. ☐

Hailstones become heavier than the air. ☐

Heavy hailstones fall to the ground. ☐

Water drops freeze and form hailstones. ☐

Another layer of ice forms on the hailstones. ☐

Small hailstones start to fall. ☐

4 Complete the puzzle. Write the secret word.

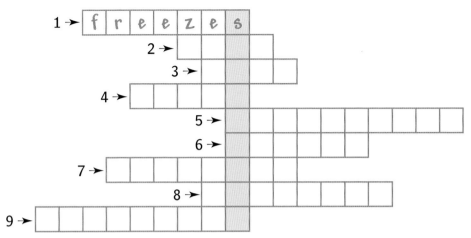

1 → | f | r | e | e | z | e | s |

2 →

3 →

4 →

5 →

6 →

7 →

8 →

9 →

1 Water __ below 0 degrees centigrade.
2 Rain changes into this below 0 degrees centigrade.
3 If your fingers get very cold, they can go __.
4 If the temperature near the ground is above 0 degrees centigrade, snow changes into __.
5 When water drops freeze high up in the air they form __.
6 In a whiteout, __ can crash.
7 When you can't see where the sky meets the ground, it's called a __.
8 A heavy snowstorm is called a __.
9 A lot of snow that falls down mountains.

The secret word is:

5 Write about blizzards. Use these words.

whiteout   cover   power cables   cars
fall down   buildings   electricity

_____

_____

_____

6 Hot Weather

← Read pages 24–27.

1 Correct the sentences.

1 Weather is coldest in places near the equator.

_____

2 Places with more than 25 centimeters of rain are called deserts.

_____

3 Winds in the desert blow from the ocean to the land.

_____

4 Nights in the desert can be very hot.

_____

5 The Atacama Desert once had no sunlight for 400 years.

_____

2 What happens in a drought? Write *true* or *false*.

1 There is no water.   __true__

2 Rivers and lakes dry up.   _____

3 There is heavy rain.   _____

4 Trees become dry.   _____

5 There is lots of food.   _____

6 Crops can't grow.   _____

3 Find and write the hot weather words.

h	d	e	s	e	r	t	r	t
o	s	w	e	a	t	c	a	f
f	i	r	e	t	q	u	d	a
s	a	n	d	s	t	o	r	m
h	h	s	h	o	v	t	y	i
u	u	u	h	o	t	e	n	n
m	n	n	t	h	o	e	p	e
s	h	u	m	i	d	f	i	r
a	r	d	r	o	u	g	h	t
f	x	a	v	e	e	l	s	z
y	a	o	q	g	u	d	l	f

1 _desert_

2 s

3 s

4 h

5 h

6 f

7 s

8 d

9 f

10 d

4 Answer the questions.

1 What can happen after a hot day in the desert?

_____

2 How high are most sandstorms?

_____

3 How long can sandstorms last?

_____

4 What do we call the amount of water vapor in the air?

_____

5 Why can't people cool down in hot weather?

_____

7 Windy Weather

← Read pages 28–31.

1 Write the words

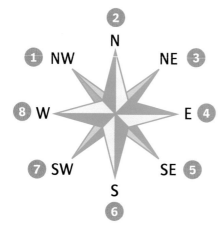

1 _north-west_

2 _____

3 _____

4 _____

5 _____

6 _____

7 _____

8 _____

2 Complete the chart.

> 3 light breeze 15 strong breeze storm
> 118 fresh gale hurricane 35 81

The Beaufort Scale			
0	calm = 0 kph	7	moderate gale = 56 kph
1	light air = _____ kph	8	_____ = 68 kph
2	_____ = 9 kph	9	strong gale = _____ kph
3	gentle breeze = _____ kph	10	whole gale = 94 kph
4	moderate breeze = 25 kph	11	_____ = 110 kph
5	fresh breeze = _____ kph	12	_____ = _____ kph
6	_____ = 45 kph		

3 Write *hurricane* or *tornado*.

1 starts as a thunderstorm   _____

2 spins down from a thundercloud   _____

3 is also called a twister   _____

4 is also called a cyclone   _____

5 can last for a week   _____

6 only lasts a few minutes   _____

7 the fastest winds on Earth   _____

8 has a center called an eye   _____

9 is like a funnel   _____

10 can change direction very quickly _____

4 Complete the sentences.

> buildings   ground   things   Australia
> cars   house   damage   road

1 Strong winds can _____ a lot of _____ .

2 A level 1 tornado can push _____ off the _____ .

3 A level 5 tornado can lift a _____ off the _____ .

4 Level 5 hurricanes can destroy _____ .

5 A big hurricane can be as big as _____ .

5 Write about storms in your country.

_____

_____

_____

8 In the Future

← Read pages 32–35.

1 Circle the correct words.

1 Earth's climate is getting **warmer** / **colder**.

2 Scientists think that it's getting warmer **slower** / **faster** than before.

3 The sun heats **Earth** / **the moon**.

4 Factories make too much **air** / **gas** called carbon dioxide.

5 Carbon dioxide traps the **heat** / **light**.

6 It's **bad** / **good** to trap some heat.

2 Complete the chart.

walk   levels   go   heat   less   power stations   energy
storms   droughts   bicycle   famines   warm   trees

Why is the climate changing?	What will happen in the future?	What can we do?
Factories and _____ make a lot of carbon dioxide. We are trapping too much _____ and Earth is getting too _____ .	There will be more _____ . More places will have _____ , and there could be _____. If sea _____ rise, some places could _____ underwater.	We can make _____ carbon dioxide. We can plant more _____ . We can _____ or ride a _____ . We can use green _____ .

50

3 Complete the puzzle.

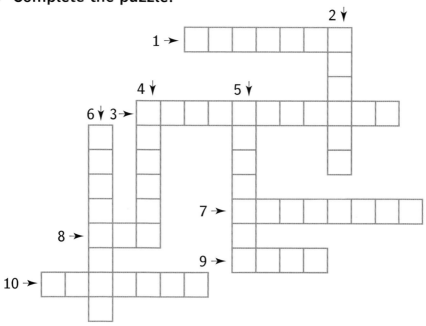

1 The usual weather for a place is its ___.
2 Green ___ makes less carbon dioxide.
3 Energy from the sun is called ___.
4 The season after winter and before summer.
5 When there's rain and sunlight at the same time you can get a ___.
6 Lots of windmills together ___.
7 A heavy snowstorm ___.
8 A thick, low cloud.
9 A lot of carbon dioxide is making Earth too ___.
10 The fastest wind on Earth.

4 Write about the weather where you live.

_____

_____

_____

A Weather Report

1 Record the weather where you live for a week. Write notes in the chart.

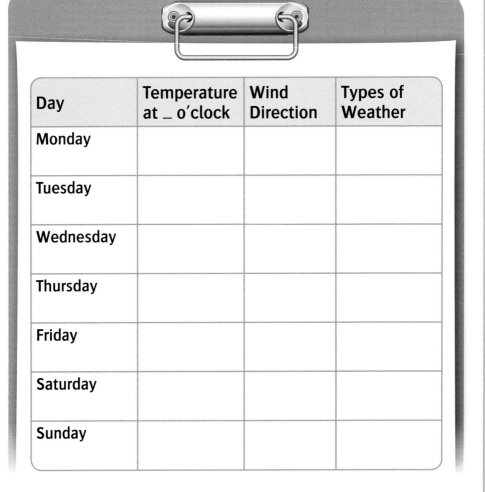

Day	Temperature at _ o'clock	Wind Direction	Types of Weather
Monday			
Tuesday			
Wednesday			
Thursday			
Friday			
Saturday			
Sunday			

2 How was the weather? Write a report.

3 Display your report.

Project 2 World Weather

1. Find some world weather information in the newspaper or on the Internet.

2. Choose a city in your country and three more cities in different countries. Then write notes.

My city:
Country:
Date:
Temperature:
Rainfall:
Other information:

City 1:
Country:
Date:
Temperature:
Rainfall:
Other information:

City 2:
Country:
Date:
Temperature:
Rainfall:
Other information:

City 3:
Country:
Date:
Temperature:
Rainfall:
Other information:

3. Write about the information. Was the weather the same or different? Which city was the hottest, the coldest, had the most rain?

4. Display your world weather information.

Glossary

amount how much there is of something

area part of a space or a place

avoid to stay away from

become to change into, to start to be

believe to think that something is true

blanket a piece of material that covers something

blow to move (for wind)

boil to heat a liquid like water until it's so hot it changes into steam

breathe to take in and let out air through your nose and mouth

breeze a light wind

bright with lots of light

calm not wild (for weather)

carry to take

center the middle

change to become different; to make something different

clear up to make clean

climate the usual type of weather in a place

coat a name for an animal's fur or skin

common usual, seen in many places

condition how something is

cool down to become cooler

cover to put something over something; to be over something

crop a plant that a farmer grows

damage to make something bad or weak

dangerous can damage something or someone

dead not living any more

destroy to damage something very badly

die to stop living

difficult not easy

direction the position something or someone moves toward

drop a very small amount of liquid

electricity a type of energy

energy we need energy to move and grow

enough how much we want or need

escape to get away from something

evaporate to change from liquid into gas (for example when water changes into steam)

famine when there isn't enough food for a long time

far not near

flash a bright light that shines for a very short time

flood where there is a lot of water where it is usually dry

forest a place with a lot of trees

form to make or be made

freeze to be less than 0 degrees centigrade; to change into ice

fresh strong and cold (for wind)

frozen so cold that it is very hard

gale a strong wind

gas it's not a solid or a liquid; like air

gentle not very strong (for weather)

glacier a large amount of ice, formed by snow in mountains

ground the land that we stand on

grow to get bigger

half one of two parts

heat something that is hot; to make something hot

humid warm and wet

hurricane a very strong wind

ice crystal a small piece of ice

icy very cold, made of ice

information what you know about something

inland far from the ocean

kill to make something or someone die

lake a big area of water

last to happen for an amount of time

leaf (*plural* **leaves**) the flat green part of a plant

lightning a flash of very bright light in the sky, made by electricity

lost when you don't know where you are

low not high

measure to find out how big or small something is

melt to make something so hot that it changes into a liquid

mild not too hot or too cold

mixture different things together

moderate between light and strong (for wind)

move to go from one place to another

mud wet soil

nature all plants, animals, and things that are not made by people

noise a loud sound

numb so cold that you can't feel anything

ocean the salt water that covers most of Earth

once one time

overflow to rise over the top of something (for a liquid)

park ranger someone who works in a park

past many years ago

plant to put plants or seeds in the soil to make them grow

power to use energy to make something move or work

power cable it carries electricity from place to place

power station a building where electricity is made

predict to say what will happen

problem something that is difficult

process when things happen one after another

protect to keep safe from danger

push down to make something move down

push up to make something move up

reach to get to

record to write down what happens

rise to go up

river water on land that goes to the ocean

rock a very hard, natural material

root the part of a plant that holds it in the soil

safely not being damaged

satellite a machine that goes into space

sea level how high the water is in the sea or ocean

second it measures time; there are 60 seconds in a minute

seed what a plant grows from

shape for example, circle, square, triangle

sheep (*plural* **sheep**) an animal used for meat and wool

sky (*plural* **skies**) where the clouds and sun are

soil the ground that plants grow in

solar from the sun

spin to turn around quickly

steam the hot gas that water makes when it boils

store to keep something to use later

storm very bad weather

strength how strong something is

suck up to lift something up into the air

survive to live

sweat water that comes out of our bodies when we get very hot

temperature how hot or cold something is

thick not thin

tiny very small

trap to keep something in a place where it can't escape

vacuum cleaner a machine that picks up dust and dirt from floors

vehicle something for transporting goods or people

warn to tell people when something bad is going to happen

way how to do something

weather forecaster someone who tells us how the weather will be

whole all of something

without not having something; not doing something

Oxford Read and Discover

Series Editor: Hazel Geatches • CLIL Adviser: John Clegg

Oxford Read and Discover graded readers are at six levels, for students from age 6 and older. They cover many topics within three subject areas, and support English across the curriculum, or Content and Language Integrated Learning (CLIL).

Available for each reader:
• Audio CD Pack (book & audio CD)
• Activity Book

Teaching notes & CLIL guidance: www.oup.com/elt/teacher/readanddiscover

Level \ Subject Area	The World of Science & Technology	The Natural World	The World of Arts & Social Studies
1 300 headwords	• Eyes • Fruit • Trees • Wheels	• At the Beach • In the Sky • Wild Cats • Young Animals	• Art • Schools
2 450 headwords	• Electricity • Plastic • Sunny and Rainy • Your Body	• Camouflage • Earth • Farms • In the Mountains	• Cities • Jobs
3 600 headwords	• How We Make Products • Sound and Music • Super Structures • Your Five Senses	• Amazing Minibeasts • Animals in the Air • Life in Rainforests • Wonderful Water	• Festivals Around the World • Free Time Around the World
4 750 headwords	• All About Plants • How to Stay Healthy • Machines Then and Now • Why We Recycle	• All About Desert Life • All About Ocean Life • Animals at Night • Incredible Earth	• Animals in Art • Wonders of the Past
5 900 headwords	• Materials to Products • Medicine Then and Now • Transportation Then and Now • Wild Weather	• All About Islands • Animal Life Cycles • Exploring Our World • Great Migrations	• Homes Around the World • Our World in Art
6 1,050 headwords	• Cells and Microbes • Clothes Then and Now • Incredible Energy • Your Amazing Body	• All About Space • Caring for Our Planet • Earth Then and Now • Wonderful Ecosystems	• Food Around the World • Helping Around the World